MW00714299

ONE THAT GOT AWAY

9 February 2002

By Saundra O. Weston

Copyright © 2001

Printed in the United States of America

Sunray Printing Solutions, Incorporated

St. Cloud, Minnesota   1-800-253-8808

The cover was designed by Saundra O. Weston.

ISBN 0-9717764-0-7

For additional copies please contact Saundra at:

Saundra Weston

P.O. Box 7615

St. Cloud, MN 56302-7615

This book is dedicated to my son, who has been with me through most of these things and is truly a child of God. I thank God for giving him to me when man had said that I could never have a child, God said I could. He is my joy and I love him very much and hope that he will forever trust and depend upon the Lord as his Father and his Friend. I hope that he will put his confidence in him and never leave him but forever depend on him and look to him for his strength and direction in life.

To my mother who I have always loved and will always love. She is the only one who believed that there was something that the Lord needed to do for me. She is the only one who believed that God could help me when the things mentioned in this book began. I love her very much and I thank God for her.

To my husband, Michael, he is my friend, companion, lover, husband, fellow minister in the Gospel of Jesus Christ. I thank God that he kept me in St Cloud, MN long enough for us to be married. He has been there for me through many things and I know that he will always be there for me. I love him and I will always be there for him. He is a strong man of God and a sincere person before the Lord. His love for people is expressed each day as he ministers to those that are homeless and to those who have come from prison. He has helped me to complete this book and to get it published and marketed for you to read.

Saundra Olivia Weston

Table of Contents

Chapter 1 Born Abroad 6
Chapter 2 My Teen Years 11
Chapter 3 Married at Twenty-One 18
Chapter 4 The First Near Death Experience 26
Chapter 5 The Second Near Death Experience 31
Chapter 6 Stripped of Almost Everything 39
Chapter 7 Time To Return To The Lord 45
Chapter 8 God's Grace Is Sufficient 53
Chapter 9 Spiritual Oppression 61
Chapter 10 God's Way of Answering Prayer 67
Chapter 11 God's Purpose Shown 73
POEMS 82
A CHILD IS BORN 82
A CELEBRATION OF PRAISE 83
ANOTHER CHRISTMAS 83
WHAT IS A CHILD 85
TEENS 86
A MOTHER'S LOVE 87
Conclusion 88

Chapter 1 Born Abroad

I was born at La Chapelle Saint Mesmin in Loiret, France on September 23, 1954. I have had various spiritual & natural experiences from the day that I was birthed until my present existence. I am the fourth child of my mother and father, a girl, who was not suppose to have been a girl if parents were able to select what gender they preferred for their children. However, it was not left up to my mother or my father what gender I was to be, it was in the plan of God that I be a girl. My mother and my father were divorced when I was very young. My mother admitted that she did not want me when I was born because I was a girl. This had an effect on me growing up and it took a long time for me to get over it. My brothers use to kid around with this and tease me; I never really realized that it was true until she admitted it.

As a child I was very quiet and often lonely, I was shy in some ways and in others just not comfortable around other people. One reason was, I had some physical disabilities and I was teased about them in school for a number of years. When I was six years old, my older brother called himself fixing me some medicine to make me feel better. I remember him bringing me a glass with a liquid in it that looked like Coke soda. Not knowing to question his actions, I began to drink it and because it tasted horrible, I stopped. I later found out that he had mixed some of the products from under the kitchen sink in a pan on the stove and it burned a hole in the pan. I got a high fever and my teeth turned yellow, my mother took me to the doctor and he gave me some medicine to help me. I didn't drink enough to do too much else from what he could tell, I believe that this is the cause of some of my medical problems that I have had to endure. My mother of course didn't blame him for doing this she blamed me for drinking it. I was only six years old, he was ten, how was I to know that what he told me was not correct. I was teased by some of the kids in my neighborhood and kids at school, even some of the children at the church we attended teased me. This very act affected the outcome of most of my life, what man wanted a woman with yellow teeth. I tried to have this covered up through different dentists, however I could never really get it taken away, neither did I find out that drinking that stuff is what caused my teeth to turn yellow until I was in my late 20's.

The only thing that I remember about kindergarten is learning to read and write when the teacher would show us (the class) the alphabets and we would have to say and write them. My mother, brothers, and I would sit in the living room and we would have prayer and Bible reading. My mother bought us a set of Bible books, the kind that told about the Old Testament stories with pictures. Each book told a story about one of the Bible characters and the things pertaining to that person or group of people. We would each read some and my mother would explain the story to us. It has been stated time and time again that parents should take time to read to their children. There should be equal time given to the children's literary needs as well as their physical needs. I remember attending vacation Bible school as a child with my brothers & my sister. This was a two-week Bible learning session where children would attend for 4 hours a day. We would study different Bible lessons and then the administrators would feed us lunch and send us home.

Vacation Bible school is one activity that is still being held today around the country. There are several Bible camps that children can attend instead of the vacation Bible school where they can stay for one – two weeks at a time. I really feel that this type of literary experience is very helpful to children. I know that it has helped me a lot and if I had been more focused in elementary school it could have helped me even more. I hope that vacation Bible school and the Bible camp's will always be around.

I grew up in a church environment, I was not allowed to go to the movies, wear pants, see boys, go bowling, go skating, wear jewelry, or do anything that was really fun. It was the way our pastor, which was also my uncle, taught us. As I began to get older I developed a desire to want to do some of those things. I would sneak out of the house when my mother was at work (as most of us who were sheltered from the world did) and participate in some of the very things that we were taught not to do. I was never given a reason that satisfied my curiosity as to why these things were not to be tolerated. So I wanted to experience them for myself. I wanted someone to love me because I felt that my mother didn't because she wanted a boy and not a girl and she never let me forget that either.

When I was in the fourth grade I remember some of us skipping school and going to an abandoned house. We would play strip poker, at the time I thought that we were just playing a game. I never realized that I was doing something that would later affect my life. I began to let boys feel on my breast and I thought that that was also OK. There was this girl who took my boyfriend from me or so I thought was my boyfriend when I was around 11 years old and I began to hate her. So one day I sat down outside and I was so mad at her that I focused all of my energy toward her and I began beating her in the head with a garbage can lid. I am not really sure if that is why I began to hate her so, I know that she did something to me that really made me mad. I was not the type of child that got mad at others easily. This is when I first realized that I had such power within me to do harm to others. I was beginning to develop my mind to do what I felt that I couldn't do physically. I didn't know that it was really working until later.

My mother never told me these things were not right, in fact she never told me anything until I started my menstruation somewhere around 12 years old. She made me mark on the calendar when my menstruation came, I was very irregular and I would miss months at a time. She looked at the calendar one day and took me into the bedroom and told me that I had better not be pregnant. I was 12 years old and had been sheltered from the things of the world. I didn't even know how to get pregnant. I didn't even know what a virgin was at that age. She took me to the doctor and this was my first physical examination. I remember I hated it, and sometimes I still hate it. It turned out that I was anemic, and a very serious one which began to show later in my life.

I traveled a lot with my church and when we traveled I would always daydream about something, sometimes I would wonder what it would be like to be the only child or have a different mother. I have three older brothers and one younger sister. My mother and I didn't have a close relationship when I was growing up. This is probably one of the reasons why I don't remember a lot about her reading to me or helping me with my homework. As I rode in the car (or on the church bus) when we were going on trips, I would read the road signs. Whenever I was in a car going somewhere I would always gaze out the window and find a road sign to read. I wanted to improve my reading to show my mother and everybody else that I was just as smart as the rest of the kids. I don't know why I felt the need to prove this, however, I just did. I didn't really like English and History when I was attending (what was then called junior high and senior high) school, because it seemed too boring.

Even though I liked to read Bible stories, I didn't know that the Bible stories I had learned as a child were connected to our society's history. This is an area that should be brought out more in our schools today if it is not being done. I believe that if the children today know the relationship of history to the Bible they will become more interested in learning about the history of our country. I really was not interested in what was really going on in the world, because I had created my own little world and I would not let anybody else in.

Chapter 2 *My Teen Years*

Being raised in the church environment and really sheltered from the world. I began to take note of what the preacher would say concerning God. We had six week revivals during the wintertime and during one of those revivals I decided that I wanted to be saved. I had began a curiosity about God and at the age of 15 I asked the assistant pastor if I could be baptized. I asked her during church service one night because I figured that if I asked my mother, she would have said no. After I was baptized I received the Holy Ghost (or Holy Spirit), or I could have received it before I got baptized, I really am not sure. All I know is that something happened to me and I was different. I really was sincere about my salvation and my walk with the Lord. I didn't really understand everything that had happened to me and I really was not prepared for what was to happen to me.

My mother was the superintendent of Sunday School at the church we attended, so we had to be on time for Sunday School. I'll never understand why, but for some reason there was always a shortage of Sunday School teachers, so I was elected to be a teacher of the small children. At the age of 15 I taught the preschool age children and our classroom was in the office of the church, because there weren't that many children. My Bible reading as a child helped me a lot when I began to teach these children. I would read to them and have them repeat what I said to see if they were paying attention. My church was a member of a larger organization know as "The Original

Glorious Church of God In Christ", and my uncle was elected as the overseeing bishop. This put pressure on us to be the best when it came time for the youth meetings and the Bible quizzes. These meetings were held once a year and we would study a particular Bible book such as I Timothy or Galatians. I always participated in the Bible quizzes.

I would read the book that has been selected for the quiz over and over and study as hard as I could. When it came time for the quiz we were all excited and we would win. We took the first place trophy for at least five to six years straight. At Christmas and Easter we would have to learn plays and remember Bible verses. One particular Easter we put on a play called "Jesus on Trial" I had to be around 14 years old. I was the defense attorney and I studied my lines very hard and everyone said that the play was the best one ever performed at the church. I was (as we saw it) dating one of the young men at our church, my cousin knew that I really liked him. She had an affair with him and she was married at the time. This really affected me mentally, because I couldn't understand how she could do that and say that she was saved.

I was always the youth teacher at every church I attended, even after I became an adult and moved away from home. At 16 I heard the call of God for me to go into the ministry of preaching and teaching His word. We were going to a revival at one of the churches in our organization located in Chillicothe, Ohio. It was during a service in the revival that I believe the Lord spoke to me and told me to preach and teach His word. I was surprised and frightened at the same time. I knew that my mother would not believe me, because she never believed what I would say to her. I was not the type of child that always told lies; I was too scared of God to tell lies. Not that I never lied, I did only when I felt that I had no other choice. But I really was scared of what God's word said, and I would always try not to be found in a position where I would have to lie. So when God spoke to me I kept it to myself for the next four years.

I was in and out of the hospital every other year during my teens. I had various bladder infections, and trouble with my stomach. I also had a lot of problems with my female organs. I began to prophesy during this time about things that were going to happen to me. In 1978 I prophesied that the next time I would be in the hospital it would be to have surgery. I had that surgery two years later in February 1980. The church always taught that we speak these things into existence, but I believe that some of the things that I said were in fact prophesies concerning my life. I didn't understand what was happening to me. I just knew that I began to know things and the things that I knew were being manifested.

I only stayed saved for that senior year of school. When I graduated at 16, I remember saying that I wanted to know what the world was all about. To this day I can see God take a stand back and cross His arms and say OK go ahead. It was the worst thing that I could have ever asked to have happen to me. My father passed away in March following my graduation. I graduated in June 1972 and he passed away on March 27, 1973 exactly seven days before his birthday, he would have turned 46 years old on April 3, 1973. When he passed I had three dreams about him coming to get my sister and me.

Each time the dream was the same, he had on a white suit and he was driving his white Cadillac. Each time he would knock on the door and when I got to the door I would look out to see who it was and I saw him, before I could open the door I would wake up. I told my mother about the dream and that I had had it three times in a row. She said that he was afraid of dying and wanted someone to go with him so he was coming to get me and my sister.

I began to date boys because I had graduated from high school and I was 16, so my mother decided to let me go out at night but I had to be in by 11. I was working full time, I had money and I began to know a lot of men, I began to drink and smoke cigarettes. What I didn't know was that I was still a virgin at the age of 16 years old. I dated my son's father for a couple of years and we broke up, he knew that I was a virgin but he never mentioned it to me. I lost my virginity when I began to date a man who was 45 years old and I was 17 and I fell in love, so I thought, it was really lust. I drove up to visit him once he had left Columbus, Ohio and returned home to Logan, West Virginia. He was of course not really interested in me in any other way than sexually.

I started dating a friend of my brothers', they played in a band together and traveled to different places within the state of Ohio. I got pregnant by him and it had been my first time being with him. When my mother found out she was furious and demanded that I was going to be put away in an orphanage. I was 17 years old and I decided that I would only be there for one year because when I turned 18 they had to let me go. Three months had passed and I was working at a shoe store as a sales clerk and it was around Christmas time. I bought my mother a stereo and I had to carry it from the bus stop to the house. I believe that this is what caused me to start having pains and I had a miscarriage, an experience that I will never forget. I was at home by myself when I started losing the baby; I went into the bathroom and sat on the toilet. I was only 17 and I had no clue as to what to do. I let the fetus fall into the commode and I screamed as the flesh from the fetus tore away from my body. The pain was excruciating, sometimes when I think about that day I can feel the pain all over again. When I was finished I called my mother at work, she of course got upset with me and came home and took me to the hospital. The hospital called my doctor and he performed a DNC to clean out my vagina from the remains of the fetus. The doctor told me after this that I would never again have any children.

I moved out of my mother's house when I turned 18 and moved in with whom I thought was my best friend. We would get high smoking marijuana with some male friends and another girl friend of ours. My need escalated to uppers and downers and many other types of pills. I began to take every kind of drug I was introduced to. Black beauties, Microdots, Valiums, Purple Haze, Orange Sunshine, and other drugs, some that I can't even remember the names of, thank God. It was living at this place where I was first introduced to rape. There was a friend of the girl that I was living with whose boyfriend was interested in me. One late night he asked me if I wanted to go for a ride and I like a fool said sure. He took me to a place way out in the country.

He pulled in front of a pool of water, which looked like a small lake and told me that if I didn't have sex with him he was going to drown me in the water. I couldn't swim and I gave in to him and had sex with him in the back seat of his car. After he finished he took me back to the apartment and we began to have sexual relations frequently. I moved out from my friend and got my own apartment. I was working two jobs and I could afford the place, I had bought furniture and I was doing well.

I never believed in Tarot cards or witchcraft or those things. However, one night after I had begun dating another guy, I was taken to his friend's house who lived in the same apartment complex where I had stayed. This guy and his girlfriend were really into Tarot cards and reading palms. Well, even though I didn't believe in those things I let him read some cards to me. He said that I was going to lose some money over the next few days. I let the guy I was dating stay there from time to time and he had a key to get in. Well, I was very naive and he stole money from my wallet when we were out one night. We stopped at this restaurant and my wallet fell on the floor in the car. He went through it and stole my money. When I returned to the car he acted like I had dropped my wallet outside the car and I must have lost it somewhere.

Some days later I had placed my rent money in the bottom drawer of my dresser. When I went to get it to pay the rent it was gone and it was the only thing missing from the apartment. I knew he had to have taken it because nothing else was missing. I approached him about it and of course he denied it, I stopped seeing him after that.

Chapter 3 Married at Twenty-One

It was sometime later that I hooked up with my son's dad again, my first husband, Ron. We dated for a total of six years before we married and he taught me a lot of things. He taught me about cars and guns and about cocaine.

Before Ron and I married I moved back home with my mother and I began to smoke marijuana in the house. One day my mother came home from church and I was in the bathroom in the tub. I had grown tired of her disbelieving me so I decided to give her something to believe in. I rolled a joint and lit it up while I was in the tub. I laid my head back against the back of the tub and puffed away. I opened the window before I lit it, however, it did not take the smell away. When my mother came home she was furious and demanded that I leave.

I moved to another apartment with another friend that I worked with (she was really a friend). I experienced a lot of depression because of the relationship with my mother and having low self-esteem, one day it got to me. I tried my first attempt at suicide. Although it seemed like things were going well for me, I was not happy and I swallowed a mixture of very strong pain pills. Both Ron and Linda were gone and I was home alone. They were strong enough to have knocked me out but nothing happened. I believe that God was saving me from myself. I never told anyone that I had tried to take my life until I got saved and began to teach young people. I felt that if I shared some of my experiences with them then they would see that they were not alone in the world and that they were not the only ones who experienced things of this nature.

Ron had introduced me to snorting cocaine and some other types of drugs. I was really getting an education of what the world was really all about. In spite of the upbringing I received about marriage and living with the opposite sex, I let Ron stay with me for a few months. I asked Linda did she mind and she said no. I could not stand the conviction on my heart from the Bible teaching that I had received as a child. So I told Ron that he had to move or we would have to get married.

We got married June 27, 1975. I was 21 and he was 23, I was six months pregnant and my child's dad and I were to be married. I feel that it was God's will for my son not to have been a bastard. As I fore stated when I was in my teens I was in the hospital every other year for a bladder infection or some type of problem with my female organs. After the miscarriage I prayed and asked God to please let me just have one child, since I was told that I would never be able to have any kids. God heard my prayer and knew that I would give that child back to Him and He let me have that one child.

After Ron and I married the next day he changed and this is the literal truth: he told me that he was an angel of the devil and that was when all of the trouble began to start and things began to get worse for me. I left him six months after we were married and stayed for two weeks Rodney was only two months old. He called me and I returned home because I believed that when you marry you marry for life. This was what I was taught in the church and what I believed in my heart.

Well things didn't turn out the way I had hoped and I left him again 1 week before our 1st anniversary. I didn't go back until four years. During those four years I experienced some very serious situations. I became a drug dealer; I would buy marijuana by the ounce every week and sell it to anyone who had the money. I became well known in the city that I lived. I had been out drinking one night and I ran a red light and the police tried to get me to pull over, I knew that if I stopped that I was going to jail, I had never been in jail before. I decided to take flight. I had a 1972-Ford LTD 2-door convertible it was blue and I thought that I could out run the police. So when he tried to stop me I took off and I am so glad that there weren't any other cars on the road that night. I finally pulled into someone's drive-way and turned my lights off. I thought that he didn't see me, but he did and he pulled in behind me and pulled his gun and told me to get out of the car and put my hands on top of the car.

I got out of the car and he handcuffed me and put me into his car. He then searched my car and found the marijuana. I was taken to the county jail and strip searched. It was one of the worst times in my life. I got 15 days for that little excursion. I was charged with five counts, fleeing the police, driving under the influence, driving with an expired license, possession of drugs, and resisting arrest. This was the first time my name was put in the paper and I was really embarrassed. My job didn't fire me, however, and I thank God again for watching over me. I always tried to keep these things from my son. I would let him spend the night over a friend's house or the babysitter's house. This time I couldn't keep this from him. My older brother was staying in Elyria then and he took care of my son for me while I was in jail. I took a lot of time with my son during the week after that. I would play with him and take him places, but on the weekends usually one night during the weekend I had to go out and get drunk and party so I thought.

We were living about 2.5 hours away from Columbus, Ohio during this time and it was 1977. I had not had any spiritual experiences up till now and I thought that God had turned His back on me for good. I thought that I was destined to die and go to hell. I had a vision one night about heaven, I had been involved in an accident and I saw myself getting out of a car on the passenger's side. As I began to rise from the car I started walking towards a field and I saw a place where there were people with white on and tables filled with all kinds of fresh fruits and other foods. I never saw anyone's face though. I walked toward the people and I remember seeing them eating and talking with one another. I soon woke up after that. I have always wondered about that vision. After having that vision, I was traveling to Columbus to pick up my aunt she wanted to come up and visit us and I was traveling on Route 301 from Elyria, OH.

There had been some trouble in the little town that I had to pass through. Some black kids had caused some trouble and I guess the people there were trying to take it out on any black person they saw. There was this man on a huge tractor and as I was going around a curve he tried to run me off the road. I thought about that vision that I had had, but I knew that I could not die then because I was not saved and I would not go to heaven. And the vision I saw was about those who had made it into heaven. So I pulled myself together and made sure that he didn't succeed in running me off the road. When I returned from Columbus, I went a different way and I didn't take that route anymore unless I had no other choice.

I was almost a victim of gang rape in 1979, it seems that a reputation had been created for me because I liked men and it was misunderstood about what I would do for any of them. Of course I was kind of loose and I liked to party but I still had some morals about myself. I lived in a basement apartment in a low-income complex. So this one night when all these boys and men surrounded my apartment, I called the guy I was dating who happened to be married, he came over and brought me a gun. I put the gun on the table and I sat on the sofa. I opened the curtain a little so I could watch them and they could see that I had a gun. I was going to shoot some of them and I was going to kill myself if they had tried to break in. That was their plan, to break into my apartment and run a train on me. I had sent my son upstairs to this girl's house that would baby-sit for me sometimes because I had heard that there was going to be some trouble and I didn't want him to be hurt. She knew what they were going to do but she wouldn't tell me. They stayed around my apartment for the next two weeks. Some of them watching me and talking about me.

My cousin had come over the next day and she had a reputation of someone you didn't want to mess with. So they didn't bother me because they saw the gun that night and they saw her the next day and every day after that for two weeks. I really thank God that that didn't happen, because I would not have survived that night.

When I stayed in that apartment, one night I was standing up and I felt something touch me on the left side. It felt like someone just touched my hip. I have had a problem with that side every since that night. It kind of scared me, but I just played it off, like I usually did when something happened that I could not explain. I moved out of that apartment into a townhouse, which I shared with this girl who was dating my brother. He moved to California and was going to send for her and her kids, so I stayed with her until they were to leave.

I went out one night to celebrate my birthday, I was driving from Elyria to Oberlin and I got drunk in Oberlin. On my way back home I was stopped by the police, he told me to get out of the car and put my head back and touch my nose after extending my arms out. Well, of course I failed that test as well as the test of walking a straight line. When he saw that it was my birthday from my driver's license he let me go and gave me a warning. I promised him that I was going straight home, well I lied and I went to an after hours place where a boyfriend of mine was. I remember side swiping a car soon after the policeman left, but I didn't stop for that.

Chapter 4   The First Near Death Experience

It was 1979 and I joined a church and accepted the call of God in my life. I preached my first message from Isaiah 6:8 Lord I Will Go. That same night I went home and had a sexual relationship with a married man. I really felt bad after that, I thought that I had something when really I didn't. After that night I never preached again until 1987 when I moved to Milwaukee, Wisconsin.

October 2, 1980 I had an abdominal hysterectomy; I had been experiencing bleeding 14 days out of the month and extreme pain. I was like this for two years before I decided to see a physician. I knew I was sick but I was tired of the doctors and the hospitals. Also I knew that I would have to have surgery, I had prophesied it earlier in my life. I had prophesied it in my teens that the next time I would go to the hospital it would be more serious. I was diagnosed with carcinoma insitu of the cervix, which is known as cervical cancer. 24 hours after that surgery I was diagnosed with Intra-Abdominal Hemorrhaging, so they rushed me back to surgery and estimated my total blood loss at 1,000 cc.

I was 25 years old when this happened and I was not interested in turning my life back over to the Lord. I had not quite finished everything I wanted to do. Plus I still thought that God had given up on me and that it would be useless to try and return to Him. I never thought about the dream that I had had when my father passed. It was not until later that I would find out that the dream was beginning to take shape in reality. The fact that I almost died is proof of the first attempt of my father coming to get me.

I continued to do drugs after I recovered and I worked very hard. I worked two eight hour jobs at one point, trying to keep ahead of the bills and make sure my son had proper clothing & shoes to wear. I also wanted him to enjoy some of life, something that I never did as a child. I never tried to get child support from his dad, because I always felt that he would not pay, and I didn't want to have him put in jail. So I tried to tough it out by myself. Rodney's dad finally got in touch with me and came to visit us one summer. Rodney was six years old, it was 1981. He talked me into moving back to Columbus, Ohio with him and trying to make another attempt at salvaging our marriage. So I being raised with the Christian ethics and beliefs that I had, agreed. Not knowing what was really waiting for me in Columbus, Ohio.

I moved to the west side of town into an apartment complex. I was working for a company called Roxanne Laboratories. I was always blessed to find good jobs, and I know that God was always watching over me because I really was ignorant, and didn't know what I was doing with my life. I went to church one night and I felt convicted and I tried to give my life back to the Lord. When I returned home that night, Ron came over and he was very upset for some reason. I let him in the house and he had a large stick in his hand. I walked into the kitchen and fixed a cup of coffee. While I was fixing my coffee he walked over to the kitchen and stood outside the door against the wall and just looked at me. I looked at the stick and then at him, he spoke and said I am not going to hit you with this. I looked back at my coffee and I said I know that you aren't. Then he left and I knew that we would never be together again. I guess the four-year separation had a lot to do with that. I didn't keep my commitment to the Lord after that night. Although I know that it was God that protected me from getting hit that night.

I started getting deeper and deeper in something that I had no idea of what was happening. I started with the drugs again and I began to work two jobs for a short time and I took care of Rodney as best as I could. I still refused to seek for child support from his dad because I felt that he would not pay. I began to receive things in the mail that asked for money and said that it could help me to get rich. Well I was skeptical about a lot of things and some of them I tried and some of them I didn't. While staying in the basement apartment of that building complex, I met several of my neighbors. One time this woman began to take all of the little children to the store and offer them candy. Of course my son didn't want to be left out, well little did I know her real intention was to get to me. It was all a trick of the devil to try and trap me. I soon became suspicious of her real intention and I stopped him from talking to her or taking anything from her.

One day I was in my apartment when I heard some talking outside, I looked out of the window, and I saw a lot of people standing in front of my building exactly in front of my window. I was not trying to hear what they were saying but I did hear some of what they were saying. This continued for a few days and I tried to ignore them but they would not leave me alone. It seems that they were talking about me. I began to get sick often, I would hyperventilate and not be able to breathe. A number of times I was rushed to the hospital and the doctors told me that if I continued that I could die. The depression never left me and I soon wanted to hyperventilate so that I could die.

As I looked out the window one day while they were out there I saw a man as tall as a light pole. I looked at him because he was so tall, he had on a sky blue suit and he was very thin. I looked over toward the left and I saw what looked like a man coming out of the ground. He had on a black shirt and black pants and he was very nice looking with a close haircut. I watched him and I heard one of the women say to him "she saw you" and he responded. "That's OK, I want her to see me". After that I turned away from the window and I began to get frightened. I didn't know why they were outside my window and what they wanted. I ended up going to the hospital that same night. I called my mother frantically and she came and took me to the hospital. I tried to tell her about the people outside my window but she never believed me. She took me to a psychiatrist and he wanted to have me committed to a hospital.

I refused to allow them to put me away and begin to pump me with pills. They tried to say that I was schizophrenic which is saying that I was unable to carry out my daily tasks and that I was having abnormal thinking, feelings and behavior. I began to hear voices in my head soon after that. I wasn't crazy, I knew exactly what I saw and what I heard. My mother began to believe me and she was not sure of what exactly was going on. She took me over to my uncle's house; he was the pastor of our Church. I told him what had happened and there was a visiting Pastor there from India, they laughed at me and I suppose they thought that I was crazy also. They left the room and I stayed there for a while sitting with my Aunt, she had been sick for some time and we just sat there. I began to speak in tongues and as I spoke she just sat there and prayed. When my mother came back to get me I left and I will never forget how, my aunt didn't stop me from speaking or ever said anything negative about that day.

After that day I was afraid to stay in my apartment, so I looked for another place to stay. When I would go out and come back there was always someone watching me. I went to work one day and I was in the bathroom, for sometime I had been hearing the voices at home and I didn't hear them at work. So this particular day I was in the bathroom at work, and I heard these heavenly voices singing. It was the most beautiful sound that I had ever heard. Soon after that I began to hear the voices 24 hours a day. It got so bad that I couldn't sleep I began to go out and I would drink because I didn't want to sleep or dream.

Chapter 5   *The Second Near Death Experience*

I remember moving out from the apartments and staying with my sister-in-law, she was buying a house on Dexter Dr. She had three bedrooms and a full basement; I moved my stuff into her basement and slept down there for a while. She then moved me into her son's bedroom and Rodney and I each had our own bed. Her third bedroom was setup as a den. It was in this house that I really became aware of what was beginning to happen to me. I started hearing birds chirping at nighttime. I never had heard birds chirp at nighttime before. I thought that was strange, I didn't tell anyone what I was hearing, I was too scared. I didn't even tell my sister-in-law.

One night I was watching TV in the den and I heard a knock on the window. It scared me, I looked at the window but I never said anything to anyone. Then when I would be sleeping in the bed sometimes the bed would move. One time the end of the bed was raised up in the air and let back down. I didn't know what it was but I figured that it had to be evil spirits after me. I had begun to hear them in my head all the time, they continued day and night.

They always would try and tell me what to say or what to do. I tried to ignore them a lot of the time, but it was very hard, they even came in my sleep. I began to have bad dreams and sometimes they were so bad that I didn't want to dream. During this time I really wasn't trying to live a save life. I had not given my life back to the Lord I was trying to figure out what was going on with me. It was also during this time that I began to actually see them I realized that I could communicate with these spirits that were talking in my head. So I began to listen to them and say things back to them and I even got into a confrontation with them. I didn't understand how I could do this but I did. One day when I was in the basement of my sister-in-laws house I saw an old white man's face. So I asked my sister-in-law who was the previous owner of the house and she told me some old white man. She said that he had died, I told her that I saw him.

My mother got mad at me because I told my sister-in-law that, she said that I shouldn't have told her that. I began to feel that my mother never really believed me or that I was going through anything, I felt that she always thought that I was making it up or that I was losing my mind. One day my sister-in-law and I went shopping downtown, she had parked the car and we were going to cross the street. We had to wait for the light and while waiting for the light to change so we could cross the street a maroon Cadillac passed by and the person inside waved, so my sister-in-law waved back. I told her that she should not be waving at strangers, after saying that, I heard in my head a voice say, "I was waving at you". I watched the car drive away. I never told my sister-in-law what I had heard. I never told her about the voices that I heard day & night in my head, she would not have understood. I didn't understand, so I knew she wouldn't. It was shortly after these events that I found a place on the north side of town. I moved my son into another low-income apartment complex. It was not any better than the first one I stayed in after returning to Columbus in 1981.

I was always fortunate to get a good job and to have a nice car. I was dating this guy who had just got out of jail and was my brother-in-law's uncle. He told me that he knew that we were going to be together while he was still in jail, this was before he had ever met me. When we were together I had began to smoke crack cocaine. This drug makes you very possessive and selfish. I had gone with my brother-in-law one day to purchase some and I told him that we should not tell Jewell about it. He went back and told him what I had said and when he came home he began to beat on me. He knocked me down and began to kick me in the back. My brother-in-law came in and saw him and asked him to stop. Jewell stopped and I got up crying and I never again tried to keep anything like that from him. Shortly after that incident I tried to commit suicide again. I took a bottle of pain pills that I had gotten from the doctor. Jewell and another friend of ours came into the house and I was in the process of passing out, when he saw the bottle and picked me up and took me to St. Anthony Hospital's emergency room.

While there an orderly or someone examined me and put some horrible smelling stuff in front of my nose to wake me up. Then he began to pinch my shoulders and he was talking nasty to me and said you should not have been trying to kill yourself. They pumped my stomach and sent me home several hours later. We were together on and off for three years, I almost

33

married him, but it was not God's will for that to be. We broke up and I was meeting new men. And I had met a new guy and I wanted to have my first blind date.

On Friday February 22, 1985 close to 5:00pm my sister and I made plans to celebrate her job promotion. I also had previous plans for that evening. We decided to make a few stops after work for a quick drink, then I would take her to pick up her girls from the baby sitter's and then take them home. I was then going to get ready for a date, which was planned earlier that week. My son at that time was staying over his friend's house so I didn't have to worry about picking him up.

My sister and I had made one stop after work downtown for a quick drink. We left there and went to another bar where my oldest brother's girlfriend worked. I didn't like her too much, because she and my brother were always fighting and she was much older than he was. We just didn't really see eye to eye on things. However, I tried to be friends with her, but she was one of those sneaky kind of people. I really believe to this day that she slipped a micky (or had someone do it) in my drink; I really didn't want to go to that bar.

My sister is three years and nine months younger than I am and I usually let her have her way depending on what's going on, she's my only sister. So we went to the bar, the time was going on 7:00pm, it began raining outside and I was really anxious to leave to go and meet this new man I briefly met earlier during the week. We finally left and I was driving. I had a black two door 1984 Plymouth Horizon hatchback, which I bought new, so it was just over a year old. By this time I had had at least two drinks. I didn't want to drink too much because I was still planning on going out. I remember getting on the freeway (I-70 North) and trying to change lanes to go west to pick up my nieces. I remember it raining very hard and there was not a lot of traffic. The rest of this is being written by the leading of the Holy Spirit, because this is the point where I lost my memory. I'm told that it was raining very hard, and visibility was extremely bad. In trying to change lanes, I hit the median on the driver's side and skid down the freeway against it for about a mile. The impact was so hard that the front half of the car broke completely off. The steering column pierced a hole in my heart, I hit the steering wheel with my mouth breaking my jaw on both sides, and my head hit the windshield. My sister's head hit the windshield also, however, she was not injured in any other way except for some scratches.

My sister got out of the car and started screaming for someone to stop to help us. Someone called an ambulance, it arrived and they had to cut me out of the car. The following is the discharge summary concerning that accident:

> "This 30 year old black female was brought into the Grant Medical Center clinically dead, after a motor vehicle accident where her chest hit the steering wheel and her head hit the windshield. On arrival, her heart rate was 104/minute. There

was no blood pressure, no pulse. Abdominal tap was negative and pupils were fixed but not dilated. The left chest was opened and showed a rush of blood. She was taken immediately to OR for exploration.

The physical examination read: Showed no vital signs. Head showed a bruise on the right forehead. She was intubated immediately. The chest showed no pneumothorax. She did have good breath sounds with bagging. Abdominal exam was negative. There were no extremity fractures on examination. Jugular venous distention was present at approximately 3 cm. With central venous pressure of 31. The impression at that time was cardiac tamponade and she was rushed immediately to the Operating Room.

The hospital course stated: She had surgery as soon as she came in and the right atrial appendage was noted to be ruptured; this was repaired and over sewn. Bilateral chest tubes were put in place and also mediastinal tube. She was closed and echocardiogram was done four days postop and showed normal echocardiogram. Multiple consults were made out to Dr. M Chen, Dr. D. Tetirick, Dr. A. Miller and to Neurosurgery for their participation. Dr. Miller was called for the facial trauma and performed surgery on 2/28. At that time, she performed extraction of the left lower 1st and 2nd molar teeth and open reduction and internal fixation of bilateral mandibular fracture using interosgeous wiring technique and application of arch bars and intermaxillary fixation. The patient did well postop and although she was clinically dead on arrival she recovered quite well and on discharge still had her jaw wired. However she was eating puree food and seemed in good spirits."

They contacted my mother and brothers and through all of this God was watching over me. He positioned the best doctors on staff at Grant Memorial to be there for my surgeries. Even though they had just come off of 12 to 16 hour duties. Once on the operating table my heart stopped again, this time for a longer period and my lungs collapsed. God enabled me to read the surgery report and it is stated that my heart stopped on the operating table for 1:21 minutes. The doctors said that was long enough for me to have become a vegetable. The doctors told my mother that she should start making funeral arrangements because they did not expect me to live. I was in intensive care for ten days and I had a concussion so I do not remember those ten days at all. I remember being taken to my room, and this is when I finally came to myself.

They didn't want me to look in a mirror because my face was so swollen I didn't look like myself. They could not stop me from looking in the mirror and I remember saying that I looked like a Mr. Potato Head. When I was being rolled into my room there were all kinds of plants and flowers and there were cards taped to the walls. I never realized that so many people were concerned about me. I really do thank them for their prayers and their support. I still did not think about the dreams that I had experienced when my father had passed away until I started writing this book. I can relate the car accident to those dreams and I understand the purpose behind his coming to me. I understand why I had the dream three times also, I have had surgery two times and two times I have almost died. If the dream is in relation to my leaving this world, then I should be having surgery or in a situation where I might die again and he will once again try to take me away.

I believe that he will not succeed because God is in control of my life and I cannot leave here until He says it's time and I do believe that when I leave this world I will go to be with the Lord. The same night of that accident there were two other females that died in a car accident in Columbus, OH. I believe that God spared our lives and the lives of those two women were taken in our place. This is the third time that I have been mentioned in the newspaper. This accident was so bad that it was written about in the newspaper. As I began to recover so speedily the doctors stated that they knew there must be a God. My trauma was not quite over though, I had my mouth wired for eight weeks, and the normal is six. I had surgery three times on the left side of my neck because of an infection where the surgery for my jaw was performed. I had three tubes in my abdomen, but God was healing me each day and I got stronger and stronger.

Chapter 6   *Stripped of Almost Everything*

I still had not given my life back to the Lord. I remember telling my cousin that I could not give my life back to God on my sick bed because it wasn't in my heart. I thank God for His mercy and grace. God of course healed me again, and I went back to my drugs and partying until this last time when I almost lost my life and a friend of mine almost lost hers because of me. I got out of the hospital and returned to work in May following the accident. I was staying with the same man we had gotten back together and I had started smoking cocaine & crack again. By having had heart surgery I should never have been smoking crack because it affects the heart. We had just smoked with a guy whose heart exploded from smoking the stuff and it still didn't stop me.

There were times when I felt like my heart was going to explode, but God was with me in that He didn't allow it to be so. I did this for 17 months after my surgery, I was trying to get away from this but I was not having any success. One day I picked up this book my brother had given me a few years back. He wasn't saved either and was not aware of what he had given me. I began to read it not knowing it was about God. I became more and more interested in that book. I tried reading my Bible and I started praying to God. Knowing that He would not hear a sinner's prayer because of the way I was taught except that it was a prayer of repentance. Somehow I hoped that He would hear me crying out. By this time in my life I felt that God had completely left me, but I didn't want to believe that. I put my Bible on my bed when I slept so I could remember to read it, but it didn't help a lot. I was hooked on crack and I could not get away. I was still hearing the voices in my head and before I had the last accident, they told me that they were going to make me have an accident and try to kill me. I thank God for watching over me and sending His angels to keep me from leaving this world at that time.

While I was sleeping one night I was awaken by something. I turned over and I saw a figure lying in the bed next to me, it raised up and it was very cold, it was dark and dead looking. As it rose up, it disappeared out of the room. I turned over and went back to sleep as if nothing had happened. I didn't want to seem like I really saw anything, I just wanted it to go away. My boyfriend and I continued to do drugs and I worked as a data entry person for a company that entered checks. We were paid according to our keystrokes. I always tried to do the best that I could, even though I had began to get high during the week as well as the weekend. My son stayed at the babysitter's most of the time, because I didn't want him to see me getting high. I was in the bed sleeping and I woke up and saw figures standing around my bed, with robes on and hoods on their heads. I remember hearing them saying something but I could not make out what they were saying. I really didn't try to listen I wanted to pretend that they really weren't there or that I was dreaming. I never told anyone about these things because I believed that no one would listen to me. I know that it was not the drugs because these things happened when I was in bed and I was not getting high at the time.

I had met a friend and we would get high together, one time we were getting high and her boyfriend was looking for her. I persuaded her to not answer the door and maybe he would go away. He was banging on the door, we were at my apartment, and we just let him bang. He soon left and we continued to get high. A few minutes later he came back, and we didn't realize it but he had went and got his gun. He had an Uzi, some kind of machine gun. We decided to open the door and saw the gun and he told us that if we had not opened the door he was going to start shooting. Again I thank God for watching over me. He pulled her out of the apartment and threw her down the steps (I stayed on the third floor) and kept throwing her all the way back to their apartment. I had learned my lesson from staying on the bottom floors and letting people stay over me. I still feel bad about her getting hurt like that, he broke her leg and she had to be rushed to the hospital and was in a cast for several weeks. I just kept telling her how sorry I was for getting her in so much trouble. I was always the type of person that it only took one time for me when something like that happened and I never again would allow anyone to get hurt because of me.

By November 1986 I had changed jobs and I was so hooked on crack that I was beginning to lose everything I had. I really believe God spared me because He does not see as man sees, He sees what's deep within a person. He saw that if He could just get my attention He would be able to change my life and I would love Him forever out of a pure heart. So God prepared a way of escape for me. I was 32 years old and my son was 11. I still tried to read my Bible and pray to God, although it was not doing me any good, so I thought. I continued to do drugs and it got to the point that I was going to be evicted from my apartment. I had quit my job at Roxanne Laboratories where I worked for five years because I was planning to move to Washington D.C., but my brother would not let me come at that time. He said that he was not ready for me to come. So I had to find somewhere else to go. I was not going to leave my son behind I had planned to take him with me because I didn't feel that anyone would take care of him in the way that he should have been taken care of and I wanted to keep him with me. Not knowing that he was my reason for going on and trying to get myself straight. If he had not been with me there is no telling where I would be today.

I had never before been evicted from any place that I lived. When the sheriff put the eviction notice on my door, I packed my bags within the next few days and I was planning to go somewhere, where I had no idea. It was the week following Christmas Day 1986, my mother came over and got me, she stayed in a one-bedroom apartment and told me that I couldn't stay there. I washed my clothes at her apartment and I was preparing to leave that same night to go somewhere, where I did not know. I had asked an aunt of mine if I could stay with her for a few days until I was able to get a place, she stayed by herself and had three bedrooms. She had changed two of the rooms into one large bedroom but I didn't know that until later. However, she wouldn't let me stay there either. So I went with my mother to her apartment and washed my clothes and packed them and was planning on walking somewhere that night. My mother went into her bedroom and shut the door.

Being directed by God, she called my brother and his wife who lived in Milwaukee and told them what had happened and what I was planning on doing. They said that if I really wanted to get my life together that I could come to Milwaukee. I said OK and my mother took her money she was saving from the bank and purchased a bus ticket for us. She took me over to the aunt's house that sat with me that day after I had come from the psychiatrist office. My uncle had passed by that time and my Aunt was bed ridden. She gave me 10.00 to have some money for food. My son and I took the Greyhound bus to Milwaukee, Wisconsin that same night and my brother & his wife picked us up at the bus station nine hours later. I was happy to have been able to get away from the drugs and the people who influenced me to do drugs. I was happy to have gotten away from the guy I was staying with also.

I thought that God had given up on me because things got so bad. But He was working for my interest all the time. On the bus trip I really believe God rehabilitated me and dried my blood up from the drugs and began to wash me inwardly. After arriving in Milwaukee, WI I told my sister-in-law that I was not going to church for New Year's, I didn't like going to church just to go. My having been saved as a teen, I knew that if I went I would be convicted and would feel bad, so I stayed away until I felt that I was ready to go back. I went to church the Sunday after New Years, I got up that morning and began to get ready, I smoked a cigarette and it made me sick. I put it out and tried to smoke another, it made me sick. I put that one out and decided to just put the cigarettes into my purse and take them with me. When the pastor had finished preaching I felt that I had escaped the conviction that I just knew I would feel.

I thought that he was getting ready to dismiss the service, when he turned and said "will the lady in the green blouse stand up", I stood up and began to cry before he even started ministering to me. He told me that it was time for me to come home. I began to cry and he prayed for me and I have never turned my back on God since that day. From that day forward God has been the head of my life and He has blessed me and healed me and kept me, and encouraged me. He has given me revelation in His word and leads me each day.

Chapter 7   Time To Return To The Lord

The week following New Year's January 1987, I typed ten resumes, put them in envelopes and put them on the couch in front of me and prayed to God before I left the house to look for a job. I received a call from a company that was small and did international business. They wanted to hire me and start me at 13,000 a year. I also received a call from Blue Cross & Blue Shield United of Wisconsin. Blue Cross was the first place I went to apply for a job, they wanted me to start at 9,000 a year. When I received the phone calls, I got on my knees and prayed and asked God to lead me. I wanted to make sure that I was being led by His Spirit and take the job that He wanted me to have. God blessed me with the job at Blue Cross & Blue Shield, two weeks after I arrived in Milwaukee. I started on January 19, 1987 and I worked for them 12 years.

After six months on the job I received a promotion and a raise. Six months later I received another promotion and raise. By the third year there I was making well over 13,000 a year, I knew that this was the position God had prepared for me. I still was hearing the voices, and every chance I got I would get in a prayer line and ask God to deliver me. I was delivered from the cigarettes, drugs, and the men, however I was not delivered from the voices in my head or the depression that I often felt. I loved God and I wanted to live for Him. I wanted to do every-thing right and be the best Christian that I could be. I wanted to be the perfect role model for my son and others.

February 1987 an evangelist came to run a revival at our church. When she finished preaching she called me out and told me that God was going to bless me, she said "A fathers' gift to his daughter. During that same service she spoke about my first house, she said that it was white and yellow and had a white fence. The Saturday night before the revival started I had a dream, I saw myself in a white wedding dress and a man's face appeared and said, "It is so". I have always believed that the person I saw was Moses. I only saw his face and he had a long white beard and his hair was completely white. Although I had never seen a picture of Moses, I just believed that that's who I saw and that is who spoke to me. Some years later I had an opportunity to see a statue of Moses I just stared at it, it looked exactly like the face I saw in my dream. When the evangelist spoke to me I remembered the dream I had the night before.

I had purchased some daily bread cards, scriptures that you pull and read each day. I would always pull a card from my daily bread and read it before I would leave for work. I was getting tired of the voices it had been going on for several years now. The Lord put me on a fast for six months'. One weekend a month I would fast, the taste for food just left me and I could not eat. I did not understand what was happening but I wanted to be obedient to the Lord so I made every effort to listen to His Spirit. During one week I pulled the same scripture for several days straight. It was II Corinthians 12:9; "My grace is sufficient for thee..." I just wanted God to help me, I thought that He was not helping me because of something that I had done or not done, but He was showing me and teaching me some thing's.

About 18 months later God spoke to me after I had prayed for His deliverance and asked me what had I learned about my enemy from this experience. I had not thought about my situation in that way I was always too busy trying to figure out why it was happening. After the Lord spoke those words to me I began to think about what He said. I realized that I had learned a lot about the way the enemy attacks and his devises. Things that are of vital importance when doing battle with the enemy. I learned that evil spirits cannot take your mind if you keep it on the Lord. A person can have complete control over what takes place in their thoughts if they allow God's Spirit to guide them into all truths. As the Bible says that the Spirit of the Lord will do.

The Lord blessed me with my own apartment in March 1987, I had left something's in Columbus, OH that I was able to store at my Aunts' house before I was evicted. Two of the brothers from the church volunteered to take me back to pick up those things. We left on a Friday night after one of them had just come off work. The drive to Columbus, OH was a 7-8 hour ride and could be done in less time depending on how fast one drove. They both sat in the front and I sat in the back, at this time I was so filled with God's Spirit that all I wanted to do was to gaze out the window and see His glory in the skies and in everything I saw. Since it was night I often would look at the clouds and the stars.

I remember first noticing that the moon seemed out of place. I had never seen it sitting where it was before. I looked and just kept looking at it, then I realized that God had moved it to light up the road for the brothers so that they could see and not fall asleep. The moon looked like it was sitting on the ground maybe 5,000 feet away from us. It followed us until daybreak and then it seemed to move back into its place.

After returning to Milwaukee from picking up my things, during a service I couldn't wait to tell what God had done for us. I never was afraid to tell about the different things that I would see and experience because I knew that God was in control of my life then and I was excited about what He was showing me. So I testified about the moon being next to us all the way until it was day-break. After service one of the brothers came up to me and said, "you know I saw that too but I was too scared to say anything". Well I just laughed and told him that I was glad that he said that because, I was not ashamed of telling about the mysteries of God but it made me feel good to know that some-one else saw this miracle also.

I began to preach and teach and I assisted with the youth department. My first year at Lighthouse Church was a year of growth for me. I didn't have a bed for my son and I went to a furniture company called United Furniture. I applied for a loan to purchase a set of bunk beds. I was turned down. I was at work on the day that I found out that they turned me down and I went into the bathroom. No one else was in there and I just cried like a baby. The Lord spoke to me and said, "I just want to bless you". I stopped crying and wiped my eyes and went back out to my desk. I never tried to purchase any beds after that. I met this man later he was about 20 years older than I was, I had started seeing him a lot. However, I was sincere about the Lord and this man had began to affect me. I started seeing him regularly. He began to buy me things and give me money. I was not having any sexual relationship with him; he just began to give me things. He was always around. He began to start asking me about having sex. I knew that if I did that it would change my walk with the Lord and I didn't want that to happen.

There was something about this man that kept drawing me to him. God used him to buy a bed for my son, God used him to bless me. I began to really like him and I did not realize that he had other motives. One night I decided to lay down with him, when I got into the bed I felt the Holy Spirit leave me. I stopped immediately and told him that I felt it leave me. He thought I was talking about the feeling of having sex with him. I was talking about the Holy Spirit. I got up from the bed and I never did that again. He brought a book of prayers over to my house after that and gave them to me. He showed me a picture of himself and in the picture God was showing me that this man was not saved. He had a can of beer in his hand. I began to notice things about him that I didn't like. He wanted to take my son places and I began to feel threaten by that so I told him no. I broke off the relationship with him and he asked if he could still be a friend with my son I told him no. After buying my first house he brought a coat to my house one day and wanted me to give it to Rodney. When he brought the coat into the house I could smell something strange.

Rodney tried on the coat and I just played dumb. I acted like we would accept it and as soon as he left I took the coat and threw it in the trash outside. He was trying to work some kind of evil upon my son and I thank God that He gave me discernment to recognize what was happening. He finally stopped bothering us. He told me one day that his intention was toward someone else, however, I got in the way. Later I heard that he had done the same thing to another lady. It seems that he liked preying on single women with boys.

The summer of 1988 I started a prayer service on Wednesdays being directed by God, and I would walk to service because I didn't have a car. On one occasion during prayer only the pastor and I was there. I was standing in front of the altar and praying. I felt a touch on the same spot on my left side where I was touched when I lived in that basement apartment in 1979. Again I didn't say anything I looked up and the pastor was in the pulpit and I could hear him so I knew it wasn't him and there was no one else there physically. It had to be the same being that touched me when I lived in Elyria, OH. I remember walking to prayer service one Wednesday, and my legs began to hurt. I got to the church and got down on my knees, I had to get up because they were hurting so bad, I sat on the bench and I cried out to the Lord, that I was not going to leave until He touched me. He healed me then and I have never had that pain again.

God blessed me with a 1978 Ford Fairmont wagon, it was a three speed. I never owned a stick before in my life. I had not tried to even drive since my brother who was a year older than I had tried to teach me when I was 16. The Lord taught me how to drive that car and I was driving the pastor and some of the members around within two weeks. I continued to have dreams and visions from time to time and this one particular instance I had a vision about three women, I was one of them, we were in my apartment and I had left the room to go into the kitchen. When I was returning to the living room, one of the women was talking and she began to say loudly liar liar liar. When I entered the living room there was a ball of fire that came down through the ceiling and lightly brushed against my leg. I believe that God was speaking about someone at the church who was lying.

I also believe that the reason I felt the fire was to help me to realize that this was real and when I would tell of this vision I could show the spot on my leg where the fire touched me. The skin where I felt the fire had a mark for two to three years and then it went away. I testified in service one night after that and one of the sisters came to me and told me that the Lord was talking to one of the Ladies in the church and she knew that she was lying. I'll never forget that vision.

Chapter 8 God's Grace Is Sufficient

We traveled to another church one Saturday for service, that church happened to be in Chicago, Illinois. Some of us took a van that seated 15 people. I was one of the people on that van, and as always I had to have my window seat because I never knew what the Lord was going to show me next. I always wanted to be where I could see whatever He wanted me to see. This particular time I was sitting by the window and a good friend of mine was sitting next to me. I was as always gazing out the window and I saw a large hand in the sky, first of all I turned towards my friend and she was talking so I looked back out the window and I saw the hand again. It was stretched out in a cup fashion and I could clearly see the thumb and the fingers. As I watched it, the Lord spoke to me and said that "I have you in the palm of My hand and nothing can pluck you out." When I turned again to tell my friend next to me to look at it, it had began to dissipate. I don't know, but I believe that the Lord was just reassuring me that I was OK, and that I had nothing to be afraid of.

The Lord blessed me to purchase my first home in October 1989. At this time I was only making about 13,500 at Blue Cross & Blue Shield. Exactly 30 days later He blessed me to purchase a 1989 Ford Tempo. I continued with the prayer on Wednesday's and I wanted to begin praying more because I had more privacy by having my own home. I could pray as loud as I wanted and as early as I wanted to. One day I was praying to God because I wanted to know where I was in my relationship with

Him. He showed me a kingdom; there were soldiers and a figure sitting on a throne. I believe to this day that the figure sitting on the throne was God Himself and this is His Kingdom that He was showing me. There were people standing around and on the right side of the throne there were rows of women kneeling with robes on that covered their heads as well. There was one whose robe was highlighted by a light that shown on her and the Lord let me know that, I was that person. This let me know that I was called as an intercessor.

When I first joined Lighthouse I experienced several dreams and visions during the first six months as I fasted. I had a dream one night about eating a white bird and I remember tasting the bird and it tasted good. But when I swallowed it I got sick. When I woke up that morning I still felt sick to my stomach. I asked another sister friend of mine who I often talked with, about the dream and she told me that I was being spiritually fed but it was not good meat it wasn't good for me.

On another night I dreamed and I saw a large beast, I was sitting facing this large beast. I wasn't scared of him. He stood on two feet and looked like a man but he had the face of an animal. His body was large and muscular he was dark and yet he was not fearful. I was fascinated with him, he showed me how to defeat the evil spirits, he picked one up and tore it in half in front of me and said "this is how to destroy them". I didn't understand what he meant at that time but I have grown to understand. I have tried on several occasions to tell my mother about these things and she has always tried to listen, but I have always felt that she never really believed me.

During a very high-spirited service a young girl who had had a lot of problems was praising God and as she began to dance in the spirit I saw a black figure leave her body and go out the door. I never said anything to anyone and I never saw that spirit come back in. After seeing that I continued to praise the Lord and the girl continued dancing and tears began to run down her face as she cried out to the Lord.

Another time we were having service and the pastor asked us to stand and face another person and hold their hands. I was sitting by this lady that was going through some very hard times. The pastor asked us to hold each other's hands and to pray for each other and help bear their burden. When we began to pray I opened my eyes and looked at her, I saw something lift off of her shoulders onto mine. It didn't scare me, because I had been dealing with these evil spirits for a long time. I began to realize that God had protected me and was protecting me. I really do not know what that was that lifted off of her, I always believed that it was her burdens. I always knew that God would not allow the evil spirits to do anything to me that He didn't allow. It took a long time for me to realize that, but I finally quit trying to ask somebody to help me get rid of the voices and began to ask God what I needed to do to pass this trial or test.

The house the Lord blessed me to buy is a white house with goldish yellowish color trim. The entire house had siding, in the back yard there is a white fence. It is a two-bedroom cottage; the upstairs is unfinished but is large enough for another bedroom. There is a side drive that four cars can fit in at one time. The back yard is a nice size and there are two large trees that shade the house very nicely. There originally were five large trees on the property. One had to be cut down and the other I had cut down because of the roots pushing against the foundation. The tree that had to be cut down was struck by lightning; it was on the northeast side of the house next to my bedroom.

One night it stormed badly and the lightning hit that tree. I didn't realize that the tree had been struck until sometime later, a couple of weeks later. When I saw the tree, I knew that God had once again protected me from being killed. The lightning went through the tree and would have come out on the other side. There was a hole in the tree and you could see on the opposite side that somehow the lightning was stopped. I believe that God sent His Angel to stop it with His finger before it hit the house and the bedroom where I was sleeping. Before moving to Milwaukee, WI I had a dream about the house. I dreamt that there were black birds in the trees in the back yard. I was standing in the yard and a big black bird flew towards my head. I remember ducking and screaming.

I also remember dreaming about some children standing around the fence on the outside of the yard saying something, however, I did not know what they were saying. After moving into the house one Saturday after I had prayed I went into the kitchen to make some coffee. I looked out the window and I saw all of the trees in my back yard and the neighbors, also in the park behind our houses filled with black birds. It reminded me of the dream that I had prior to moving to Milwaukee. I just looked at them and they seemed to know that I was looking at them.

The Bible says that God gave man dominion over all of the fish of the sea, and over the fowl of the air, and over every living thing that moveth upon the earth. Genesis 1:28. This was taken from man when Adam fell in the Garden of Eden, however, God gave it back to man through Noah, Genesis 9:2, after the waters had succeeded off of the face of the earth. My belief in God and His Spirit within me has enabled me to not allow these creatures to frighten me. From time to time they would often sit in these trees and sing or talk whichever it is that they do.

I had another vision during some months later, I saw a building that looked like a church and everyone in side and those that were going inside had on white. I sat on a bench in the back of the building and there were people sitting next to me on both sides and it appeared to be a service of worship & praise to God. Again I could not see any faces but I remember the place was full of people and there were people that remained outside also. The people were talking and someone was standing up in what looked like a pulpit talking. This had to be another vision of heaven or the waiting place where those that have passed away to be with the Lord are waiting for the end of days.

During my time at Lighthouse there were many prophetic words spoken to me by various ministers of the Gospel. One particular prophetess spoke concerning the salvation of a family member of mine, a male. She also told me on that same night that my sister's children were going to be reunited with mother. These things of course happened a short time later. She also spoke that I am suppose to be rich and that she saw silver and gold around my feet. Well, I have been blessed by several things and I have always thought that she was talking about natural blessings only. I failed to realize at that time that God does not only speak to the natural man, he speaks to the spiritual man as well, and usually when prophecies come they come to not only help that particular person, but they also come to help those who will be blessed through that person.

Things started changing at Lighthouse and I believed that the Lord was leading me to another church so I left. I joined a church called Temple of Holiness Deliverance Church of God. I attended this church for three years and it was at this church that I was licensed as a minister and ordained as an evangelist. After the three years had passed I was praying to God, I asked Him what did He want me to do concerning a special service that I was to put on. The Lord put into my spirit to have a Mother & Daughter dinner. We sold tickets for $7.00 and the children's were half price. Some of the people thought that $7.00 was not enough to charge, well a friend of mine was catering the meal and I was donating a certain dollar amount. I was not doing this to make money for the church, I was doing this to bring deliverance to several relationships that had been destroyed by various circumstances. I asked my mother if she would be the speaker, first she turned me down. Later she called and said that she would speak. I believe that God was using this occasion to bring us together and many other mothers' and their daughter's. The dinner was very successful and we sold all of the tickets.

The pastor had begun to make remarks that were not Godly and make insinuations that were uncalled for. She wanted things to go the way she felt that they should go, especially regarding certain personal relationships which she tried to include me. I felt that it was time for me to go I had begun to experience a lot of jealousy. When I was at Lighthouse I visited another Church and there was a prophet that was running a revival there. He told me that God wanted to make me happy and that there was going to be a lot of jealousy towards me. Well, he certainly was right.

The house that I owned had a side door that opened into the house to a small hallway, directly downstairs is the basement. Another door opened into the kitchen to the right in the hallway. I would shut that door and lock it just like I shut the outside door. One night I was sleeping and I woke up in the stage between sleep and being awake, this is where there is nothing but darkness. I looked towards the door of the bedroom because I heard a door shut. It sounded like the kitchen door. I saw a tall figure that looked like a man standing in the doorway to my bedroom; it looked like he was as tall as the door entrance. When I saw him I said Jesus real loud and he disappeared. I do not know if this was the same being that I saw outside my window when I stayed in the basement apartment in 1981/82. I turned over and I went sleep, I was no longer afraid because the Lord had given me strength and I had began to listen more to His Spirit and I wanted to be led by Him in all things. The Bible tells us that His Spirit will lead and guide us into all truth. (John 16:13)

Chapter 9   Spiritual Oppression

I went to St. Anne's Cathedral Holy Church of Deliverance and I asked God that if this was where I was suppose to be then let it come from the pastor's mouth. I did not tell anyone that I had prayed and asked this of God. I had visited this church on several occasions. One Sunday that I went to visit after the pastor finished preaching she said to me that I was going to be a member of their congregation and that God told her to ordain me again. I joined their church and worked closely with the pastor for two years. The Lord told me to drive the pastor to the church in Madison, WI on Sunday's. She had been driving down there after preaching in Milwaukee by herself mostly every Sunday. I was very nervous about this because I never wanted anyone to get close to me because I just didn't trust people that much. So I began to drive her and we began to build a relationship. Many times when the pastor would go out of town she would leave me in charge sometimes I would bring the message. Then I would travel to Madison, WI by myself to help in the service there. Sometimes I would bring the message in Madison also and sometimes I would just be there to be supportive of their service.

I began to have bad dreams again and the devil would come in my dreams, one time I had an epileptic attack. My eyes rolled back in my head and I couldn't move. I remember seeing Jesus written out in bright lights and I tried to say Jesus, however I had a hard time saying it, eventually I got it out, got out of the bed and called my pastor and asked her to pray with me. I went to the emergency room at St. Joseph's Hospital before I went into work and the doctor told me that he could not say that I didn't have an attack but that something had happened to me.

It was hard for me to go to church and minister to others and come home and face the things that I was facing. I would cry to God because sometimes my head would hurt from the voices talking and I felt that I just couldn't stand anymore. God did give me a time of peace where I heard nothing, I didn't hear any voices and it was the most beautiful sound that I had heard in a long time. I would have dreams about other people sometimes also, and I continued to have dreams and visions from God. I could not understand how God could talk to me with the voices always talking. But God being who He is, is Almighty, is never without a way of doing whatever He wants to do.

He gave me a dream one night about an old phonograph playing a record. It was one of those with the large horn on top that the sound came out of. I asked Him what the dream meant and He told me that He had put old songs down in me. I always wondered why sometimes I would know a song and I know that I had to be too young to remember the words to the song. But after the Lord explained the dream to me I understood why I would know these songs.

One time when I was sleeping something touched me, I

felt something touch my skin through my clothes. I believe it was one of the angels that watch over me, when I awoke I was not scared. I believe that the angel was waking me up because I had overslept. I was told that God had given me a special angel and sometimes I would feel a presence close to me. I could tell sometimes when the presence was evil or good that was close. Sometimes I would not try to know which it would be because I didn't want to know.

In the house when I would be in the bathroom sometimes I would hear knocking at the bathroom door, more like banging. My cousin came to visit me from Columbus, OH; it was her first time coming to Milwaukee. She was in the bathroom and I was in the kitchen I heard a loud bang on the bathroom door. I know it was that evil spirit that was in the house. I went to the bathroom door and told it to stop. My cousin never said anything about that, but I know she had to feel strange and I know she heard it. She has since passed on home to be with the Lord, so I'll never get an opportunity to ask her if she heard anything.

I would sit in the living room and watch TV and I could feel the presence of something or someone. I always looked around but I saw nothing even though I really didn't want to see anything. I knew something or someone was there because I could feel it. I was watching TV one night not long after I had moved into the house and a figure just walked in through the front door. It didn't have legs or look human it was just a figure it was white and went pass me and as it passed me I ignored it and just kept watching TV like nothing had happened. I knew that if I noticed it then I was opening it up to continue its behavior so I just ignored it.

On another occasion I was sitting in the living room watching TV and I saw a figure move in front of the living room picture window. It probably was the same spirit that came in through the door, it looked at me because I looked at it. I really believe that there was more than one spirit in the house, but I never really tried to find out how many were there. I could sense them sometimes and sometimes I could see them.

My prayer time usually was early on Saturday mornings before 6 or 7 am. I was praying one Saturday morning and I began to hear a lot of birds. I looked out of the kitchen window and the trees in my back yard, around my house and in my neighbor's yard were full of black birds. They were keeping up a lot of noise and didn't seem to be leaving anytime soon. I began to pray and to rebuke any evil that may have been released by their being there. Eventually they flew away and never did that again.

The best thing I liked about my house is that I know that God blessed me with it and He always let the sun shine on it for me. It could be a cloudy day and the weatherman may have predicted clouds for the entire day. God would let the sun peak through just long enough to shine on my house. Or shine on me wherever I was. If I were in my car the sun would shine on me each day. I took this as a sign from God showing His love for me and His promises to keep me in all of my ways.

My son had left and went to Alabama State University for college in 1994. I let his friend, which had become close with our family stay with me for a while, I treated him as if he were my own son. He also professed to be a minister and he was only 22 or 23 years old. He only stayed there for a few months and then he moved, he was not very stable. He left his furniture there for a while and I had put his recliner in the living room, it was black leather. As I was sleeping one night I saw a dark figure sitting in the recliner. I don't believe that this was a dream, I believe that it was more like that stage between sleep and being awake. Everything was dark and I could not see anything. Then I looked up and I believe that the person sitting in the chair was the devil and I yelled at him that I was tired of him and he told me that he was tired of me too.

He would come from time to time to taunt me and I was unsure why he would come until I later learned why. I really was tired of them all, but God would not stop the voices in my head or the spirits from entering into my dreams or appearing before me. I couldn't understand why I was seeing these spirits and why they were bothering me at that time. One day I finally decided to stop asking God to take them away and changed my focus of the situation. I fasted and prayed a lot and asked God to give me strength to go through. I wanted to know how to defeat them. Although I never forgot the dream God had given me with the beast showing me how to destroy them. I really didn't understand how to do that or exactly what He was trying to tell me. I got weak and tired and I began to want to give up. The Spirit of God just wouldn't let me give up, and I'm glad for that now. I do not want to give the devil any place in my life, the Bible says to give no place to the devil and that's exactly what I do not want to do.

Again while I was watching TV one day I was sitting in the chair in my living room and I felt something on my stomach. It was a spirit trying to get inside of me. But because of the Spirit of God in me, it could not get in. Nothing can hurt or harm us unless we allow it access to our flesh. No spirit in heaven or hell can enter us without our acceptance. People who are possessed have been possessed because they opened themselves up to the spirit that has taken control of their bodies. This also is scripture and it is found in Matthew 12:28-29. I should have been scared but I believe that God had been preparing me for all these things and strengthened me to go through them.

Chapter 10 God's Way of Answering Prayer

I remarried in 1996 and my then husband did not want to live the kind of life that I was living or that we were created to live before God. However, I believe to this day that God put us together. God would always show me a sign when He wanted to show me that He approved of what I was doing. We met at the church that I was attending. He had recently joined and became a member. I was preaching one Sunday and I began to minister to the people individually. I prayed for him and when I touched his head, I felt something strange. I never spoke of this to anyone because they would have just said that I was feeling my hormones because I was single. Well at that time I was not considering marrying anyone, I was only interested in doing the will of God. One of the larger churches was having a tent revival with activities in the daytime. I decided to go and while I was there I saw him there. We began to talk, we ate together and stayed together the rest of the time we were there. He began to tell me how he wanted to get married and how he had become interested in a couple of the ladies at the church. At this time in my life I had stopped trying to look sexy or available to any man, I really didn't care anymore. I didn't pick up on the fact that he was talking about me. I had even mentioned that certain one's might be good for him. I drove the pastor to Madison the Sunday after that and she began to talk about him. She said how he had talked with her and told her that he was interested in a couple of the ladies at church and was looking for a wife. She made a point of telling me that he would be very good for someone and that he knew how to make a lady feel good. She went so far as to say that if she were younger she would consider him herself.

It was June 1996 and I wanted to have some work done to my house and he had told me that he knew how to cement. I asked him to come over and look at what I wanted to have done and tell me how much he would charge. I decided to let him do the work and he began within the next few weeks. He was outside working and I came out to see how he was doing and asked if he wanted something to drink. He begin to talk about getting married again and asked me if I was ever going to remarry. I was kind of surprised and then again not. I answered yes and that some day when the right person came along it would happen. We began to see each other regularly and I told him that I did not believe in dating and that we would have to think about getting married or stop seeing one another. He came over on my birthday, September 23 and took me out to dinner at Red Lobster it was still early. After returning home he asked me to marry him, I told him that I would have to pray and see what God had to say. He didn't have a car so I took him home that night from my house and on the way to taking him home God gave me a sign. I was getting off of the freeway (94 West) at the 35th Street exit. As I began to exit to the ramp it started raining. I looked straight ahead and noticed that the rain was light and the sun was shining, when I looked toward the sky I saw two rainbows. After I reached the top of the exit ramp and stopped at the light to turn left the rain stopped and the rainbows disappeared. I didn't stop at that sign, though, I continued to pray and I had asked three other close friends of mine to pray with me about this marriage. Well, the Lord did not tell or show anyone or me that I had praying with me that this was not His will so we got married December 1, 1996.

In preparing for this wedding, I could see the hand of God in everything. The person who handled everything for me, she did an excellent job and one of my friends from work did all of the pictures for me. When my maid of honor and my son and I went to look for my dress we went to two shops. The first one we did not find anything, so we went on another side of town. The second place we went had two buildings and we went to the first one and I tried on a dress well I didn't really like it. We left there and went across the street to their other shop, and when the clerk showed me the dress she had I fell in love with it. I tried it on and it fit almost perfect. Only the tops of the shoulders had to be altered, everything else fit perfectly. The dress was originally tax included about $1,000 and I paid only about $360.00. Everyone was talking about that dress which I still have and may pass on to my granddaughter. On the day of the ceremony the church was packed. I know that several people who came came because of our friendship and others came to be nosy. There is always somebody who wants to just see what's going to happen. My mother and my brother drove up from Columbus, Ohio and my mother was in her late sixties. I was really glad that they came. We did not have sex prior to our wedding night, because I strictly believe in the word that I preach and that is that sex outside of marriage is a sin before God.

The same day we returned from our honeymoon he wanted to follow after his former ways of getting high and going out to party. He decided to take some of the money we were given and he went and got high. He wanted to change me, but I could not let him change me, because I had been through too much to allow the devil to win. I had to have him put out of the house two months after we were married because he was abusive. God told me at that time not to divorce him and I heard Him clearly although I did not understand why He had allowed me to be put into a relationship like this. I considered myself to always be prayerful and see the Lord concerning everything so that I would not have to suffer some things, namely something like this. If God had not spoken to me when He did I would have divorced him quickly. We were separated for about two to three months and I let him come back trying to give the marriage another try because of what I believed. One of the evil spirits (could have been more) that was in the house took him over and made him even more hateful than he already was.

We were in the bed making love one night and I saw a spirit rise out of him and hover in the air then it went away. I tried to tell him what was happening to him, but he would not listen or he could not listen. He started his old habits again and he attacked me again for the second time about one month after I had let him come back, this time he began to hit me in the head and choke me. He did this because he had given me 90.00 and I took it over to his mothers to keep him from getting it back to go

70

and blow on some drugs. Fifty of it belonged to his daughter who lived with her mother and I didn't want him to renege on his word. He blew all of his check and wanted the 90.00 back. He got angry when I told him that I didn't have it and he wanted to know where it was. I told him that I took it out of the house because I knew he would return for it and he began to hit me. When he left I called his mother to warn her that he was on his way over there. I also called the police, his mother and pops came over to see about me.

I didn't go to the hospital until the next day because I didn't think that I was hurt that bad, God had sheltered me from the blows I really didn't feel a thing when it was happening, and I do not remember feeling anything. I did have a black eye the next day and there were bruises on my head.

After that night I began to cry out to God and ask Him why this had to happen and He reminded me of a prayer that I had prayed some time ago. I had asked Him to give me the same kind of compassion that Jesus had when he walked the earth. God told me that this is how you get that kind of compassion, by loving someone no matter what they do to you. So I began to think about things differently. I tried again to let Larry come back and see if he wanted to change his ways. He always said the right things, but he just couldn't keep his word. I know for a fact that the spirits were controlling him. He even began to notice that something wasn't right with himself, and I had prayed that God would open his eyes and show him.

71

When he came back this time I saw a spirit turn him over from side to side, flipping him like a hamburger or something. It happened very fast and I knew that it was done for my benefit to show me that it was in control. I should have been scared to even lay down beside him, but I wasn't and I know it was because of God's presence and His Holy Spirit that lived in me. We never seemed to be able to live together as we should have been able to after these events. I lost all trust in him and anything that he said. I still wanted to be the godly wife that I had been called to be. I still refused to give any place to the devil.

I received many promotions from my job because God blessed me to be able to go to school and I received my Associate Degree in Applied Science, in Computer Science; Microcomputer Specialist. This was a very difficult time for me, because I still was not free from the voices in my head, and I would try to study and take tests and I just couldn't think sometimes. With the things that I faced with my husband and going to school not to mention the work in the ministry I felt compelled to keep up I began to wear down. I would cry and ask God to help me because I just couldn't think when taking my test at school. God helped me to graduate with a 3.65 grade point average. I became a member of the National Vocational - Technical Honor Society, I was nominated to the All American Academic Team, and I was added to the book of Who's Who Among Students in American Junior Colleges national publication. I also received the Lamp of Knowledge award. These things could not of happened with the oppression that I was dealing with 24 hours each day seven days a week without God's help.

Chapter 11 God's Purpose Shown

I was promoted to a Systems Administrator position at work this allowed me to travel to various places for meetings with other companies that had the same kind of software that we used for our life insurance policies. These meetings were to get information on the latest upgrade to the software and to meet others who might be able to help with some of the problems that we were experiencing. One of those trips took me to a place called Kiawah Island, South Carolina. On the flight there we were above 30,000 feet in the air. I remember we were above the clouds and I sat by the window. I looked out the window and I saw a road in the sky. It was not a cloud made to look like a road, it was a road like you see on the ground. I watched it until I could not see it anymore. It made me think of a lot of things concerning the Bible and how the devil is the prince of the air. I don't know where the road lead to but I'm sure that it was a road, there were clouds around it and I could tell the difference between the two.

After seeing that I just kept watching out the window. We were above the clouds and I saw a black figure, I looked at it and watched it as it came from above in the sky and descended in the direction that looked like where the road was. This figure was the size of a human being and I could see it clearly without trying to figure out what it looked like. It was too high up to have been a bird, it did not fly like a bird flies, and it was too large to have been a bird. I really do not know what it was, I know that it was not a bird.

My husband and I moved to Minnesota and tried once again to save our marriage, well he decided that he still was not ready to give up his live of drugs and partying. So we didn't last long after I moved here. He moved in January of 1999 and I did not move until June 1999.

I continued to have dreams and visions about things. I had dreams about my husband when things were not right between us. I still have dreams and visions and my desire now is to complete my work in the earth and go on to live with the Lord. I believe this is why I am in St. Cloud and before I came to St. Cloud, I visited my mother-in-law's church. The pastor that brought the message called for a prayer line. The Lord told me to go up for prayer. She prayed for me and anointed me, she said she was anointing me to complete my work.

I continued to have dreams about various people and things concerning their lives. I began to preach and whatever the Lord gave me for someone He always manifested that word. I believed that the experiences that I had in Milwaukee were over until one night when I was in the bed. I felt something in the bottom of the bed with me, it was moving towards me. I cried Jesus and it disappeared. It had to have been a spirit.

My ex-husband and I stayed together for one and a half month's and I ended up leaving him because he became abusive again. This time he had a knife in his hand and I decided that enough is enough. Although I believe that God put us together, I believe that God did not intend for me to be a punching bag and to be abused continually just to make a point to me. I left him and went to a shelter for 3-4 days. I was working and I had some money. I needed to be able to get a restraining order on him so I needed to go to the shelter in order to get it fast. While staying at the shelter I saw several women with children and some without. I took that opportunity to be a blessing to someone. I believe that if we want to allow the Spirit of God to lead us we can turn obstacles into opportunities. This is what I had begun to pray for and I received the opportunity to be a blessing in several ways. I left the shelter because they needed the space and I could afford to stay in a hotel for a few days, until the sheriff put him out of the apartment so I could return home.

The second night that I was staying in the hotel it was around two in the morning and the phone rang. It was the hotel attendant, he informed me that my husband had just signed into the hotel and that they did not want any trouble so they thought that I should know. Well I decided that since he was there I could go home and I left with the help of the attendant. They even gave him a room two doors down from mine. At the time the person who signed him in did not know that he was my husband, when the second person came back that was working (the night manager) he knew.

When I got home it was a mess. I walked into the apartment and there was garbage all over the kitchen and eating area floor. He had pissed in the bed and it was stinking. He had pawned my VCR, small TV and everything that he could carry out the door that he thought that he could get some money for. We stayed separated for a year, then I bought a house and I tried one more time to let him come back. This was the last time, he disrespected me so bad, and he had been seeing this girl ever since he came to St. Cloud in early 1999. She even attended the same church as we did. I did not find out that this was the person until after I had been called to pastor and had left the church.

I also had dreams about my ex prior to our legal separation, which was effective December 2000. God began to use me mightily and He always seemed to bless me when my husband (now ex) was not with me. I do believe that He continued to protect me and keep me and I know that His word is true.

I began pastoring Temple of Faith Church in January 2000. I prayed continually about this because I wanted to make sure of what I believed the Lord was directing me to do. He had worked everything out down to the receiving of our IRS Identification Number (EIN) and the State Tax Identification Number. The Lord picked the name of the church and we have a web site under the same name "TempleofFaith.org". It was surprising to find that no one else had even thought about using the same name. I knew then that God had already planned for Temple of

Faith to exist and has great plans for it's future in St Cloud, Minnesota.

When I moved into the house that I have now, one night shortly after I moved in I woke up early in the morning and something jumped off of the bed and ran down the hall. I always thought that it had to be a spirit, however, after some time of learning about my house I think it might have been a rabbit that found it's way into my house during the winter months. God has blessed me so that I now can handle when the spirits appear and began to trouble me. I know who I am in Christ and I know the power that is within me. I know that as it is written in the word of God that "nothing by no means can harm me." I know that I will die here and it does not scare me. I only want to finish what the Lord has written in heaven concerning me. It has not been an easy journey but I know that God is with me and that Jesus is my strength. I will stand against all evil and whenever the opportunity arises I will pull anyone I can out of the hands of the devil.

I do not expect to reunite with my ex-husband and have decided that after two years have ended I will remove my wedding rings. I want more than anything to be in the perfect will of God. There has recently been a migration of black birds around my house, this does not bother me, however, I will be watchful and prayerful, because I know that my enemy is going to and fro as a roaring lion seeking whom he may devour. There were times that I prophesied to others and I never worried whether or not the prophesy would come true, I know that God's word will never return unto Him void. I truly believe that it is the word of God that gives life and strength in time of need and that I cannot help or tell anyone anything without His Holy Spirit to guide me in all of my ways. I believe that He will continue to show me wonders and I only want to stay in the position to be able to see them and have the dreams and visions that will bring hope into someone else's life. My son is in Japan and his family is suppose to go to be with him. I have given him over to the Lord and I never took him back. I know that God will take care of them and He has enabled me to prepare for them once I have passed on.

I can thank God for bringing me through all that I have experienced and teaching me His way. I thank Him for choosing me to show His signs and wonders to. I use to be bothered by people not believing in the things that God has showed me or the things that I have experienced. Now I do not care if they do not believe me, I know that everything that I have said in this book has happened or will happen and I know that anyone who is experiencing what I have experienced can be helped if they truly want to be. They only have to give over to the Spirit of God and allow Him to help them. They do not have to be put into mental hospitals and pumped up with medicine. They can live a life free of demon oppression and sin and be victorious in many areas of their life. God did not intend for us to be put away into hospitals to be filled up with medicine and left for dead. He wants to heal all of us if we want His healing power. It is my prayer that everyone who reads this book will accept the call of God upon his or her life and in their life and not give in to the devil any longer. Stand and be counted with the saints (not the Christians). There will be Christians in hell, but there will not be any saints there. God called us saints from the beginning and I refuse to allow the enemy to call me anything other than what God has called me.

God has helped me to be able to cope with the problems of oppression that have plagued me; they are not as they were some years back. I believe that God has given me the strength to endure these things so I can be of help to many people going through similar situations. God has taught me how to fight and how my enemy fights. He has taught me how to know my enemy and that everything I need to win this battle is in His hand. The doctors would like to diagnose this type of oppression as schizophrenia. They eventually will accept the truth that it really is demonic oppression. God has helped me to see and realize that I have more power than those that are oppressing me do. They may have tried to break my spirit but they cannot do it because of the love of God inside of me.

On December 22 1999, I had another dream. This dream troubled my spirit. I was in this house with other people and nothing seemed out of place until I looked at my watch. My watch had a strange silver and fuchsia color look to it. There were no hands on it and the silver and fuchsia colors were mixed together into a point. I went into the other room and told this lady who was in there and she said that it was the mercury in my watch. I looked at a clock that was sitting against the wall and the hands were going around continuously. Then I went upstairs to another room where there was a man and a child and the television was on and the newscaster was saying how there was darkness in several places of the country. I looked out of the window and I could see the darkness coming. I could not tell what direction it was coming from just that it was coming fast. As it drew closer I could see birds, there were ducks and other types of birds or what appeared to be flying animals with faces that looked like beasts and they were the size of little children. They flew by the window closely and I could see them real clear as they passed by. The people in the house began to scream and run into different rooms. We went downstairs and one of the girls ran out the door and across the street. It seemed that these animals were not flying over the houses across the street only on our side of the street.

We told the boys that were downstairs in the basement what had happened, there were three parrots walking around and the boys were not surprised at what we were saying. As we were talking to them the sky cleared up. Then within a few seconds there appeared flying fish coming towards the house from the opposite direction of the birds. I saw snails and sea horses at the windows trying to get into the house. They were banging on the windows and the roof trying to get in. They could not get in so they flew away. Before I woke up I saw a number 2002 and I heard the Lord speak that these things are going to happen before the end of the year 2002. However, the Lord said that this is not the beginning of tribulation.

I am joining with another ministry here in St. Cloud that ministers to people who have been in prison for various reasons and the homeless. I will be working with them and continuing to pastor until God directs me to stop.

From all of the experiences written here I have been blessed to write several poems. Each poem represents a special time in my life. They are written for others who I have had the pleasure of knowing as well as my only God given son. Each poem is a part of me and expresses my feelings about the issues stated therein.

This is the first poem that I wrote, written in 1988

A CHILD IS BORN

There came from above an Angel one day
He appeared unto a woman as she sat in her own way
He told her that she would conceive a child
As she looked at him in dismay
She said but how can that be when I know not a man in that way

As he departed her she danced with glee
Then decided she must go to tell her cousin
Of this joy that she now knows

Her cousin was glad because she too had, had a visit one day
From an angel who told her she too would conceive
A joyous bundle one day

The child was born in Bethlehem
And in a manger he did lay
As Wise men, Shepherds, and all mankind
Did give to him great praise

He was born not a normal child
But one worthy to be praised
One who came to seek and save
All that could be saved

You to can meet this child who lives
If you would like to give him praise
For he is here with you and I
Even here today

This poem was written for my Pastor's retirement from her physical job 1993.

A CELEBRATION OF PRAISE

This is a time of celebration
For the natural man's labor
One day we all hope to rest
From the weary world's favor

Now we've been taught that
A time to retire is a time to rest
And this time of rest
Is the best of man's quest

Although I want to give you a thought today
Please take it
Keep it
Treasure it always

Here we are honoring a Vessel of God
Who has not just decided to sit down and rest
But to let the Spirit man pick up
Where the natural man's left

You see the purpose should be
To seek a natural rest
Only to give God the praise
By giving him your best

This poem was written for a Christmas celebration

ANOTHER CHRISTMAS

Another Christmas adons us!
 How does it affect you?
Does it make you feel like giving
 Or bringing someone good news.

Does it make you think of our Lord & Savior
 Born a very long time ago.
In a little city called Bethlehem
 In a manager all a glow.

Does it make you think selfishly
About what you want to receive
Or how you can beat someone else
Out of what they should believe

Just what is on your mind
As this day appears to us all?
Can you just once set aside your own
Desires to hear a lost soul's call?

Let's all for a moment bow our heads
And thank our Lord Jesus above
For being born so long ago
Just to save us all!

This poem was written for Easter 1988

EASTER 88'

This Easter is very different from all the others gone by
Mainly because the year that is present is near to that precious time

Where is your treasure laid up, is it in this world laden with sin?
Or is it stored in the glorious Hall of heavens great storage bins?

We know the true story of Jesus Christ who died and rose again
And why he rose to save our souls from a place where Angels were
condemned

So why not put away your worldly ways and fleshly pride
And glorify Christ Jesus our Savior for it is he that gives life

This poem was written for Easter 2000

Easter – A Celebration of Life

To every thing in it's Season
A time to live and a time to die
This is the Season for you and I

As you go through-out this day

Remember it is God's Love that was sent to save
He too was a natural man
Who had a choice to consider His own plans
And now we can see the works of His hands

He chose the way that was set before him a way not easy to endure
For a cross was his end to clear our sins

Some want to live in his footsteps for a day
But no one can know how he suffered
He suffered so very much and the way

He no longer is detained in a grave held by chains
For He lives and cleansed Mankind's sinful stain

We must also choose a way
For it is written and there is no escape
What will your choice be today?

To everything in it's Season
A time to live and a time to die
What time do you choose for your life?

This poem was written in regards to my only son as a thank you to the Lord

WHAT IS A CHILD
A child is one who really cares
A child is one who knows no fears
A child is one whose love is true
A child is one whose caress is smooth
A child is one whose hugs mean more
  Than candy from a candy store
What is a child to you and I?
  To me my child is the apple of my eye
I thank God that he blessed me so
  To have a child that he too knows

This poem was written for Rodney's 14th Birthday 11/8/89 (my son)

TEENS

I am a teen in the 89' scene
All my friends are here too
And guest what's good about that?
We're all still in school

We go to church
And sometimes we listen
But we're just to slick
To be a christain

We hear the word of God
And we should really take heed!
But for some reason
We all miss that seed

Now why is this?
Cause we're so kool
To kool sometimes
To come to Sunday School

So we lay in on Sunday's
Cause we've may have had a rough night
And that could be because we
Think we're always right

You see it's like this
We've become Teen Adults
We're those kind of people
Who are to young and to old to be taught

I must first ask myself if this is me
Cause, as I think about it
It really could be

And I want you to ask yourself
If this could be you too
And if the answer is yes
Then I suggest that you start attending Sunday School

When I asked my mother
To write me a poem
I had no ideal
What she would do

Boy am I ever glad that I go to Sunday School
Cause being a teen in the 89' scene
Is almost through

You see Sunday School will help
Us to learn more about God's word
And so we have a better chance
To be better teens in this world

So if this poem is talking about
You and you've just decided that
You want to be like us too

You should make up in your
Mind tonight to start, or continue
To attend Sunday School
Oh and by the way
I mean youth services too

The poem was written for my Pastor's Mother's birthday in September 1994

A MOTHERS LOVE

When the Lord made you he created a precious stone
A person whose life that would be sweet and long

A person who shows love, cries, and feels
One who others can depend on in times of fears

When God created you he imparted his joy, peace, and happiness
A strength that would forever flourish when you should be depressed

He made a vessel of honor from which lively stones would grow
Jewels that would shine as the stars and above others be well known

He's kept you free in his Spirit safe from many harms
To bless you and protect you until he calls you home

His love for you is strong and is given to all mankind
He'll continue to comfort you throughout the rest of your time

He's kept your mind stable and given you a song
To sing praises unto him for to him and him only do we belong

Conclusion

It is said that schizophrenia is a disease and that it cannot be cured. I do not believe that it is a disease because of the experiences detailed in the events mentioned in this book concerning my life. There are several instances in the Bible where Jesus healed those who were oppressed by demon spirits. These people probably were the same as others and myself. One might ask the questions why hasn't God healed me? Well, I do not have the answer to that and I have asked that question myself many times. I only know that I have become aware of a power that I would not have known if I had been healed ten or more years ago. I have been dealing with this since the early 1980s and I know that I have grown in the Lord to a place that I do not fear what the devil may try to do to me, or any demon spirits that he may send to attack me. I believe that God is with me in all that I do and I know that I have the victory in Christ.

After reading this book along with other facts and findings, make the determination for yourself. If you watch the prophetic word given in this book you will see that it will come to pass and you will also see that the only cure for demon oppression is a life hid in Christ. A life that has been crucified with Christ and allows the Holy Spirit to lead him/her daily. One must commit their life unto the Lord and I know he will keep their mind and bring them through every test and trial. I have not been completely set free from hearing the voices and I may not receive that until after I have left this life. I still have occasion where I can hear them and they still try to take control of my mind. However, I know that if I stay in touch with the Father, Jehova-shalom (The Lord send Peace) that I will have peace of mind for the rest of my natural days upon this earth. And I have began to understand more about how God works in our life just by having gone through a lot of the experiences that I have had. I hope that everyone who reads this book will, if they know of anyone suffering with this affliction, help that person by leading them to someone who is Spirit filled and a true believer in Christ.

Since I began to edit this book and prepare it for publishing, I have been blessed to marry a wonderful man, who is a man of God. The Lord has brought us together and without his help, love, patience, and understanding I may not have been able to continue in the way that I have been. This has been a long battle many times I have prayed for the Lord to shorten my days and let me come home. Since I have married Michael, I no longer pray that, I pray that God's perfect will be done concerning my time remaining here. If you have never experienced these things then it is hard for you to fully understand why a person would ask to leave this world. It is very stressful sometimes until a person has learned how to fully trust in the Lord God Jehova. I know that I have the victory because of who Jesus Christ is and because I have accepted Him as my Lord and Saviour. I trust that the Lord has and will continue to keep me in every way that I walk. He has blessed me and will continue to bless me for me to be a blessing unto others. I hope that you will feel the wonderworking power of God through this book and will share it with those whom the Lord leads you to. If anyone reading this book has not already found the comfort in Jesus Christ to let Him fight their battle, let Him fight it, they will be at peace and victorious. Isaiah says that the Lord will keep "...him (anyone) in perfect peace, whose mind is stayed on thee (God), because he trusteth in thee."

One That Got A Way, is a compelling testimony of the life of Pastor Saundra Weston. With a message of God's love, power, and deliverance by the Holy Spirit. She tells of the Hand of God upon a person's life. From a dysfunctional childhood of rejection to drug addition then to the symptoms of what some call Schizophrenia. This book will bring salvation and deliverance to many, pass it on. Pastor Michael Laidlaw, Executive Director of the Dream Center of St. Cloud, Founder of Overcomers International Fellowship, & Senior Pastor of Temple of Faith

In writing a foreward for this book, which has stirred a desire to walk closer to the Lord, I wondered how I could best describe Saundra. When I first met Saundra I knew from earlier conversations on the phone that she was a dedicated servant of God. So it was easy to talk to her. To listen to what God was telling her to do and then to do it. To write this book and to get the message out to as many as possible. I immediately concluded that soul winning and witnessing were the primary goals of her existence. For our Lord tells us that "he is not willing that any shall perish. But that all shall come unto repentance. To sum up my assessment of Pastor Saundra Laidlaw, I believe I can best describe the author of this book as being a woman of courage, conviction, and compassion. May this book inspire countless Christians and non-Christians to a deeper commitment and a renewed yearning to become children of God. This book will challenge all believers to be witnesses for Christ wherever God has placed them. And to go forth in God's strength to bring the light of the gospel to those around them. Russell J. Simon Jr., author of "No Way But God's Way" & "Inside the Walls"